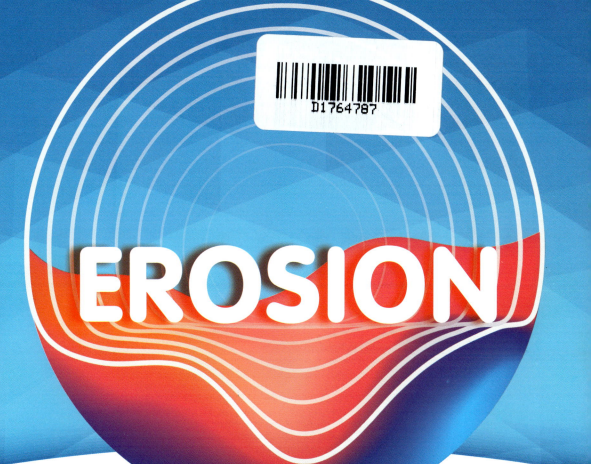

EROSION

by Tamra B. Orr

Raintree is an imprint of Capstone Global Library Limited, a company incorporated in England and Wales having its registered office at 264 Banbury Road, Oxford, OX2 7DY – Registered company number: 6695582

www.raintree.co.uk
myorders@raintree.co.uk

Edited by Charly Haley
Designed by Jake Nordby
Original illustrations © Capstone Global Library Limited 2022
Production by Joshua Olson
Originated by Capstone Global Library Ltd
Printed and bound in India

978 1 3982 0406 5 (hardback)
978 1 3982 0407 2 (paperback)

British Library Cataloguing in Publication Data
A full catalogue record for this book is available from the British Library.

Acknowledgements
We would like to thank the following for permission to reproduce photographs: iStockphoto: halbergman, 23, MaxKolmeto, 12, nantonov, 11; Shutterstock Images: Alexxxey, 9, Anek Krachangphat, 15, Anton_Ivanov, cover, Elena Arrigo, 7, Hang Dinh, 18, IrinaK, 28, Kriachko Oleksii, 24, mariyaermolaeva, 5, Salvador Maniquiz, 27, Stephen Barnes, 16, T.Fritz, 19, trekandshoot, 20, Trphotos, 8, Valentin Valkov, 17
Design Elements: Shutterstock Images

Every effort has been made to contact copyright holders of material reproduced in this book. Any omissions will be rectified in subsequent printings if notice is given to the publisher.

All the internet addresses (URLs) given in this book were valid at the time of going to press. However, due to the dynamic nature of the internet, some addresses may have changed, or sites may have changed or ceased to exist since publication. While the author and publisher regret any inconvenience this may cause readers, no responsibility for any such changes can be accepted by either the author or the publisher.

CONT[ENTS]

Words in **bold** are in the glossary.

What is erosion?

Erosion is the process of nature changing Earth. Wind blows soil away. Heat makes rocks crack and break. Rivers wear down the land they flow through. The water carries rocks and soil to new places.

Erosion is always happening. But it usually happens too slowly for us to see. It forms valleys. It shapes coastlines and mountains. It wears away everything from the tallest mountain to the longest beach. It changes the land over millions of years.

Ocean waves shape coastlines through erosion.

Where is erosion?

Erosion happens all over the world. Water changes land near oceans and lakes. Rivers change the land too. **Glaciers** are giant pieces of ice. They change the land in the coldest places on Earth. Rain and wind change land everywhere.

Oceans, lakes and rivers are found all over the world. Water shapes the land along oceans and lakes. Rivers cut through land. They also move soil and rocks.

Rivers can cut deep valleys into land.

Glaciers are in the world's coldest places. Glaciers move very slowly. They change the land when they move.

    Wind changes land that is not protected by plants and trees. This happens most in deserts. A lot of desert land is flat. There are no trees or hills. Wind blows fast across flat land. This makes huge sandstorms in deserts. The sand hits rocks. It changes the shape of the rocks.

How does erosion happen?

Many things in nature cause erosion. Water is one of these. It changes land in many ways. Ocean waves move sand on a beach. This changes the beach over time.

Rainfall hits rocks. It slowly wears them away. **Acid** in rain can make holes in rocks. Rain and snow wash away soil too. They move the soil into rivers.

Rivers flow through land. The moving water breaks up the rock and soil it touches. The rock becomes small pieces. The water carries rocks from one place to another.

Sometimes water gets into cracks in rocks. This can happen because of snow or rain. The water in the cracks can freeze. It gets bigger when it becomes ice. This makes the cracks bigger. The rocks can break apart.

Ocean water can also sink into cracks in rocks on the shore. Eventually the water dries up. It leaves behind salt. The salt can build up in the cracks. It breaks apart the rock over time. The pieces may be washed away by water. They may be blown away by wind.

Wind is another part of nature that changes land. Wind blows every day. It moves soil and rocks from one place to another. This changes the land over time. Wind is what makes tall sand **dunes** in deserts.

Wind erosion affects farms. Wind carries away the **topsoil**. Topsoil is good for plants to grow in. **Crops** won't grow well without topsoil. Farmers try to keep their land safe from erosion.

When glaciers move, they flatten land. They make valleys. They shape mountains. They gather soil and rocks as they move. This makes the glaciers heavier and faster. They can change the land more.

Hot weather changes the land too. Rocks get hot when the sun shines on them. The heat can make the rocks crack. The rocks become weaker. The rocks break into smaller pieces over time. Wind and water carry the pieces away.

A force called **gravity** also changes the land. People cannot see it. But it pulls everything towards the centre of Earth. It is why something falls to the ground when you drop it.

Gravity helps erosion because it pulls rocks and soil to the ground. This is what happens in a **landslide**. Chunks of rock or soil fall off the side of a mountain or cliff.

Why is erosion important?

Living things help erosion. Plants and animals change the land. People do too. But erosion also helps living things. It shapes the land around us.

Some beautiful landforms were made by erosion. The Grand **Canyon** in Arizona, USA, is one of these. The Colorado River dug into the land for millions of years. This made the deep canyon. The canyon is many kilometres long. Plants and animals live there. They would not have a home without erosion.

Many people visit the
Grand Canyon.

There are many ways that living things change the land. Have you ever seen a dandelion growing out of a crack in the pavement? This is an example of how plants cause erosion. Sometimes plants grow in cracks in rocks. The cracks get bigger as the plants grow. The rock breaks apart over time. Then wind or rain carries the pieces away.

Animals such as moles and gophers also change the land. They dig into the ground. This breaks up the soil. It becomes easier for rain or wind to carry the soil away.

People can also make erosion happen. They cut down forests. They move soil to build things on the land. Doing these things makes it easier for wind and rain to move the soil. This changes the land.

Erosion can be harmful or helpful. It is harmful when it damages the land we need for growing crops. But it is helpful when it makes homes for plants and animals.

Erosion is how nature changes the land. It can even create beautiful landforms over millions of years. Erosion is always happening all around us.

Glossary

acid substance that is sometimes found in water; acid can wear away rock

canyon very deep river valley

crop food plant grown in large amounts

dune sand hill made by wind

glacier huge sheet of ice found in mountain valleys or polar regions

gravity force that pulls all things towards the centre of Earth

landslide when soil and rocks fall suddenly from the side of a mountain or hill

topsoil top or surface layer of soil; topsoil is good for planting because it contains decaying leaves, grass and other organic matter

Find out more

Books

Earth's Landforms (Earth By Numbers), Nancy Dickmann (Raintree, 2019)

Mountains and Valleys (Let's Explore Britain), James Nixon (Raintree, 2018)

Rocks and Minerals (Eyewitness Workbooks), DK (DK Children, 2020)

Websites

www.bbc.co.uk/bitesize/topics/z849q6f/articles/z7w8pg8

Learn more about rivers and how they shape the land.

www.dkfindout.com/uk/earth/deserts

Find out more about deserts.

Index